PARABLES

FROM JESUS

BOOK 3

Deadra Neary

WestBow Press books may be ordered through booksellers or by contacting:

WestBow Press
A Division of Thomas Nelson & Zondervan
1663 Liberty Drive
Bloomington, IN 47403
www.westbowpress.com
844-714-3454

ISBN: 978-1-6642-9865-1 (sc)
ISBN: 978-1-6642-9866-8 (hc)
ISBN: 978-1-6642-9868-2 (e)

Library of Congress Control Number: 2023907645

Print information available on the last page.

WestBow Press rev. date: 05/02/2023

WESTBOW
PRESS®
A DIVISION OF THOMAS NELSON
& ZONDERVAN

The Faithful Servant and the Wicked Servant - Matthew 24:45-51

Servants Three - Matthew 25:14-30

DEDiCATioN

This book is dedicated to Jesus Christ, my Lord, who gave
me the inspiration and ability to write these poems.

To Caroline and Spencer Smith, who started me on this journey.

To family and friends for their love and support.

Par – a – ble

A parable is a story Jesus told for me,
teaching me how my life should be.
A faithful servant we should always be,
doing our best, God wants to see.
We should be loving, helpful, and kind.
Obeying God, we must keep in mind.
So read with me these stories so true,
from Jesus, our Savior, to me and to you.

4

The Faithful Servant and the Wicked
Servant - Matthew 24:45-51
A faithful servant the master does need--
one who is trusted and humble indeed.
The master gives him charge of what others servants do.
He watches the household and gives them their food.
The master can leave with no worries in sight.
His faithful servant will do what is right.

A wicked servant will not find trust.

Everything he does will end up like dust.

He beats other servants and withholds their food.

He eats and drinks and is always rude.

The master will return when the servants know not.

Each will be given their deserved lot.

When the master returns and finds all is well,
to his faithful servant the master will tell;
"My faithful servant so good and kind,
I trust you with all that is mine."

When the master returns, the wicked does not care,
They will pretend to be good and look prepared.
but to the wicked the master will say,
"Your life will end this very day."
While the faithful servant was granted peace,
the wicked's life will quickly cease.

12

Par – a – ble

A parable is a story Jesus told for me,
teaching me how my life shall be.
God's faithful servant works all day
helping others without delay.
Our work for God, we will enjoy,
and Satan, he can never destroy.
So read with me this story so true,
from Jesus, our Savior, to me and to you.

Servants Three - Matthew 25:14-30

There were three servants their Master did trust.

He found them all faithful, good, and just.

He went on a trip and left them His money.

What will they do while he's on his journey?

To one servant he granted five bags of gold.

The servant wheeled and dealed, and was very bold.

18

To the second he gave two bags of gold.
The servant bought and bought, and finally sold.
To the third he gave only one bag of gold.
This servant was afraid and not in control.

Then one day the Master returned,
anxious to see what His servants had earned.
The first servant came with ten bags of gold.
You gave me five now look and behold.
"Good and faithful!" the Master did sing,
"I'll put you in charge of a great many things."
To the second servant the Master did call.
"Show what you did for one and for all."
The second servant said, "I wish I had more,
instead of two, you now have four.

The Master called to the third, "What did you make?"
The servant stepped up but to only shake.
"Your money I buried deep in the ground,
so when you returned it could be found."
"How lazy you are!" said the Master point blank,
"The least you could do, was invest in the bank.
The interest alone would have interested me.
Alas, the same bag is all that I see."

So give me back that single bag of gold.
It passes to the first, for he is very bold."
The faithful servant, you see will be given more.
He loves his work. It is never a chore.

The faithless servant will be thrown outside.
In the darkness, he is destined to reside.
I hope you enjoyed these stories so true,
found in the Bible, in the pages of Matthew.

Printed in the United States
by Baker & Taylor Publisher Services